For my sister, Susanna.

Special thanks to Claudia and Philip Davis

From the author of **Paddy and the Magic Pirate Hat, Bea Gives Up Her Dummy,**
and **Tell Me About Heaven, Grandpa Rabbit!,**
winner of the *Gold Prima Baby Award* for *Best Children's Book.*

978-0-9934203-4-4   978-0-9926167-3-1   978-0-9926167-7-9

This book belongs to

....

Published in 2016 by Little Boo Publishing

ISBN: 978-0-9934203-0-6

A catalogue record of this book is available from the British Library.

little boo publishing

Ben gives up his Dummy

Written by **Jenny Album**   Illustrated by **Claire Keay**

little boo publishing

Ben had a dummy,
which he used ALL the time.

He used it in the day when he played…

He used it in the night when he went to sleep…

And sometimes, he even used it in the bath!

Then, one day, Mummy said, "Ben, you're far too old to use a dummy now. They're for little babies, not children as old as you."

"Also, dummies make your teeth stick out, so if you're not careful, you might start to look like a bunny rabbit."

Ben imagined what he would look like as a bunny rabbit – and he didn't like it very much.

Also, it was true what Mummy had said. He *was* the only one of his friends who still used a dummy.

"So what shall I do Mummy?" asked Ben.
"Give them to the Dummy Fairy of course!"
Mummy replied.

So the next day Ben and Mummy went round the
house and collected up all of his dummies.

They found a dummy at the bottom
of the toy box…

They found a dummy under the sofa cushions…

They even found a dummy underneath the piano.
(It was very dusty.)

That night Ben put all the dummies in a big brown
envelope and left it outside his
bedroom door.

Mummy told Ben that if he was a good boy and went straight to sleep with a smile on his face, he might receive something special from the Dummy Fairy the next day.

So, with a happy little smile Ben drifted off to sleep.

Later that night, Ben woke up to see a tiny fairy
sitting on his lampshade.

"Hello," said the fairy, "I'm the
Dummy Fairy, and I've come to take all of your
dummies off to Fairyland."

"Why?" said Ben.

"Well," she replied, "we fairies have lots
of uses for dummies…"

"Sometimes we use them as boats
to sail down the river."

"And the fairy children use them as roundabouts to spin round and round in the fairy playground."

"And when the weather's really bad in Fairyland, some fairies use them as umbrellas to shelter from the rain."

"Wow!" said Ben. "I didn't know that!"

Then he paused. "But Dummy Fairy…" he said.
"I know the fairies really need my dummies,
and I do want them to have them. But…er…
I still *really* want my dummy too!"

Gently the Dummy Fairy said, "Don't worry Ben, every time you start to miss your dummy, just think very hard about something you love to eat. If you do, I will magically make you *taste* that special thing in your mouth."

Then she waved her magic wand and
Ben went straight to sleep.

When he woke up, the envelope outside his door had gone. And in its place was a little present from the Dummy Fairy!

Ben was very happy.

That day, Ben didn't really miss his dummy at all.
But that night, when he went to bed, he did a bit.

So as he lay there, Ben decided to think very hard
about honey on hot buttered toast.

And guess what? Suddenly he could actually
taste the honey in his mouth.

The next night when he missed his dummy he thought about thick, creamy banana milkshake!

And the next night, he thought of…well he didn't think of anything very much really… he just fell straight to sleep.

In the corner of the room a little fairy smiled
and waved goodbye.

Her magic was done…

Lightning Source UK Ltd.
Milton Keynes UK
UKHW051226190223
417177UK00009B/69